Excel VBA Programming for Beginners

Excel VBA 2013
Make it Easy. Practical Guide

By Charlie Torrance

Table of Contents

Disclaimer

While all attempts have been made to verify the information provided in this book, the author does assume any responsibility for errors, omissions, or contrary interpretations of the subject matter contained within. The information provided in this book is for educational and entertainment purposes only. The reader is responsible for his or her own actions and the author does not accept any responsibilities for any liabilities or damages, real or perceived, resulting from the use of this information.

The trademarks that are used are without any consent, and the publication of the trademark is without permission or backing by the trademark owner. All trademarks and brands within this book are for clarifying purposes only and are the owned by the owners themselves, not affiliated with this document.

Introduction

The need for computer applications is on the rise. VBA is an easy programming language that any one can learn. It is very common in the creation of desktop applications, which are often used for management purposes. Any task that you do from Excel can be automated with VBA. You can even use the VBA for validating the data that is being entered in Excel sheets.

A good example is when you expect to receive a certain number of characters in a particular Excel sheet. You can create VBA macros to help you ensure that the user has completed certain actions before closing an Excel sheet. VBA provides developers with an excellent way for handling errors that may occur. This makes it a good programming language to learn. This book helps you learn applications development with VBA. Enjoy reading!

Chapter 1- Getting Started

VBA (Visual Basic for Applications) is a programming language that helps you to control everything in Excel. After an application has been created with the Excel VBA, it will be referred to as a "macro".

Visual Basic Editor

This is a program provided with Excel that helps us communicate with it. In this book, we will be using Microsoft Excel 2013. To launch Visual Basics Editor, first you need to open MS Excel 2013. Accessing this editor in this version of Excel can be challenging, but the steps given below will help you achieve this.

You have to use the window for "Microsoft Basic for Applications". Ensure that you are able to see the tab for "DEVELOPER" in the toolbar.

This is the tab that will provide you with the necessary buttons for opening the VBA editor and allow you to create form controls such as checkboxes, buttons and others. If you don't find this tab, follow the steps given below to open it.

From the menu bar, click on "FILE", and then click on "Options", which is located at the bottom of the drop down menu.

Info

Protect Workbook

Control what types of changes peop

Inspect Workbook

Before publishing this file, be aware
- Document properties, author's
- Content that people with disab

Versions

There are no previous versions

Browser View Options

Pick what users can see when this w

A new window will pop up. Click on the option labeled "Customize Ribbon", located on the left, and then move to the right and activate the "Developer" checkbox.

After that, click "OK". On the toolbar of the Excel window, click on the "DEVELOPER" tab. Click the option for "Visual Basic". You will see a new window pop up, which is the VBA editor.

The First Macro

Now we will create a form with a button on it. From the new window, click on "Insert" in the toolbar, and then choose "UserForm". You will see the following window pop up:

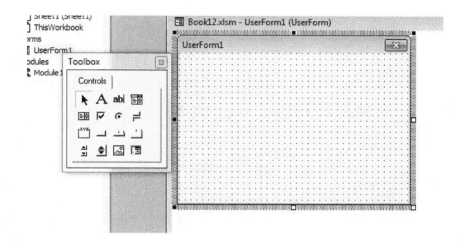

The Toolbox window has all the elements you may need when creating a form. If this window disappears, you only have to click on the "ToolBox" icon, which is shown below:

Hover your mouse over this tools window until you find the CommandButton. You just have to point to each element and their names will be shown. Drag it to the right where you have your form.

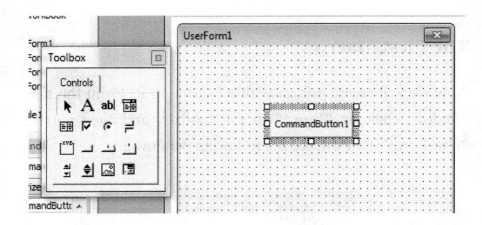

Right click on the button, and then choose "Properties". Change the "Name" and the "Caption" for the button.

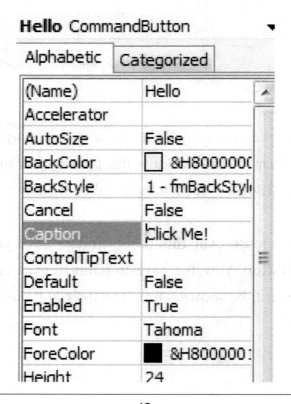

Note that the Name will uniquely identify the button, while the Caption is the text that will appear on the button.

You can then double click on the button and you will see the code responsible for creation of the button. Although all you did was drag the button, some code was generated. In my case, I get the following:

```
Hello

    Private Sub Hello_Click()

    End Sub
    |
```

We need to modify it so that once we click on the button we will get a message box with a message. Just edit the code to the following:

Private Sub Hello_Click()
        MsgBox "Hello, you have made your first Macro!"
End Sub

At this point, you can run it by clicking on the run button (▸). You will see the following:

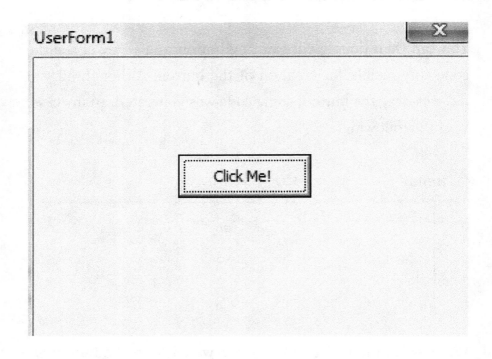

Click on the button labeled "Click Me!" You will then see the message box given below:

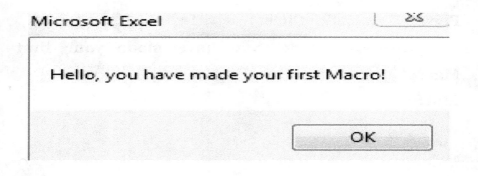

You have successfully created your first macro! Congratulations!

What we have created is a sub-procedure named "Hello_Click ()". The use of "Sub" keyword specifies that we are creating a sub-procedure. We have then used the "End" keyword to end our sub-procedure.

Modules

A module represents the area in which the code is to be written. To insert a module, you just have to click on "Insert", and then choose "Module". This will give a new window where you can write your code.

Comments

Comments are used for documenting programs to help the programmer or anyone else who may need to know the meaning of the various lines of code used in the program. During the execution, the interpreter will ignore comments. There are two ways for denoting comments in VBA:

1. By preceding or starting the statement with a single quote ('). The following two statements denote this:

'I am learning VBA
'I am enjoying it.

Those two statements will be treated like comments in VBA.

2. Preceding the statement with "REM" keyword. Consider the examples given below:

REM Written by Nicholas Samuel
REM An international programmer.

The interpreter will skip those statements, as they are comments.

Chapter 2- Variables and Data Types

Variables work in the same way as mail boxes in a post office. Similarly to mail boxes, the contents for a variable change from time to time. Variables are areas that have been allocated by a computer memory for data storage. Each variable in VBA has to be given a name.

The following are the rules you should adhere to when declaring variables in VBA:

- They must not be more than 40 characters

- They must have only numbers, letters and underscore characters

- No spacing should be used

- The variable name must not begin with number

- Period (.) is not allowed

Below are some examples of valid variable names:

My_Bike

ThisMonth

You_Can_Use_A_Long_Name

Class8

Below are some examples of invalid variable names:

My.Bike

1Year

John&Mary

Class 8

The period (.), ampersand (&) and spacing are not allowed in naming of variables in VBA.

Data Types

Excel VBA data types can be divided into two categories:

- Numeric data types
- Non-numeric data types

Numeric Data Types

These are the data types that are made up of numbers. We can apply mathematical operations such as addition, division, multiplication and others on these data types. There are 7 numeric data types in VBA, including Byte, Integer, Long, Single, Double, Currency and Decimal. All of these differ in the amount of storage space allocated to the variable.

Non-numeric Data Types

These include String, Date, Boolean, Object and Variant.

Variable Declaration

Before we can use a variable in Excel VBA, we have to declare by assigning a name and a data type to it. The declaration of these variables can be done either explicitly or implicitly.

Implicit Declaration

In implicit variable declaration, we simply use a variable and assign a value to it. The interpreters will automatically inference the type of the variable based on the value that you assign to it. Consider the examples given below:

FirstName="Nicholas"
MyAge=24

In this case, the Excel VBA will create two variables namely "FirstName" and "MyAge" and they will also be assigned their respective values.

Explicit Declaration

In implicit declaration of variables, it is easy for us to get errors. This is why we should use the explicit declaration of variables. In this case, we have to use the "Dim" keyword to declare the variables, while following the syntax given below:

Dim variableName as DataType

Consider the examples given below:

Dim yourName As String

Dim password As String

Dim num As Integer

Dim total As Integer

Dim BirthDay As Date

If you fail to specify the data type in this case, it will be declared as a Variant.

When declaring strings, you can use either fixed-length string declaration or a variable-length string declaration.

Chapter 3- Arrays in VBA

An array refers to a memory location that can store more than one value. The values stored in an array must belong to the same data type. When you use an array, values that are related can be referred to using the same name. The values or the elements of an array begin at index 0.

Declaration of Arrays

In VBA, arrays are declared by use of parenthesis (). The size of your array has to be within this parenthesis. The declaration of an array takes the following syntax:

Dim arrayName (n) as datatype

The array will have the name "arrayName" with a size of n, which represents the number of elements in the array. However, this is only a declaration for a static array, which is an array with a fixed size. These are useful when you are sure of the number of elements you will store in the array.

Dynamic arrays re used to store the elements whose number is not pre-determined. The following syntax is used to declare dynamic arrays:

Dim arrayName() as datatype
ReDim arrayName(4)

In the "Dim arrayName() as datatype" line, we are declaring an array named "arrayName", but we have not specified its size. We have used "ReDim arrayName(4)" after that to define the size of this array.

Now we need to create an example that will help you understand how to use arrays in VBA.

Begin by opening your Microsoft Excel. Save the workbook with the name "VBA_Arrays.xlsm". Ensure that you choose "Excel Macro-Enabled Workbook" from the drop down list, below where you can write the name of the file.

In this workbook, click on the "DEVELOPER" tab, then click on "Visual Basic" on the left side of the toolbar.

We want to create a user form with a single command button. Click on "Insert", and then choose "UserForm". Drag and drop a command button into the form, as we did earlier.

Click the button and then edit the Name and Caption to "Fruits" and "Show Fruits" respectively, as shown below:

Fruits CommandButton	▼
Alphabetic	Categorized

(Name)	Fruits
Accelerator	
AutoSize	False
BackColor	☐ &H8000000(
BackStyle	1 - fmBackStyl
Cancel	False
Caption	Show Fruits
ControlTipText	
Default	False
Enabled	True
Font	Tahoma
ForeColor	■ &H8000000:
Height	24

You should now have the following:

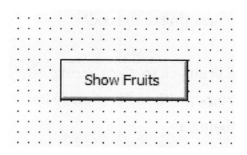

Right click on the button, then choose "View Code", or simply double click on it and you will see the code window for the button. Add the code given below to the new window:

```
Private Sub Fruits_Click()
    Dim Fruits(1 To 4) As String

    Fruits(1) = "Mango"
    Fruits(2) = "Banana"
    Fruits(3) = "Orange"
    Fruits(4) = "Others"

    Sheet1.Cells(1, 1).Value = "My Favorite Fruits"
    Sheet1.Cells(2, 1).Value = Fruits(1)
    Sheet1.Cells(3, 1).Value = Fruits(2)
    Sheet1.Cells(4, 1).Value = Fruits(3)
    Sheet1.Cells(5, 1).Value = Fruits(4)

End Sub
```

Let's explore the meaning of the code:

In the line "Dim Fruits (1 To 4) As String", we are declaring an array named "Fruits", with the first array index being 1 and the last array index being 4.

The line Fruits (1) = "Mango" helps us assign the value "Mango" to be the first element of the array. The rest of the related code does the same by assigning the different elements to the array.

The line Sheet1.Cells (1, 1).Value = "My Favorite Fruits." helps us to write the statement "My Favorite Fruits" in the cell with the address A1. We have used "Sheet1" to refer to our current sheet. The cell (1,1) is referring to the cell at the intersection of row 1 and the column 1(B).

The line "Sheet1.Cells(2, 1).Value = Fruits(1)" will help us to write the value contained in index 1 of "Fruits" array in the cell at the intersection of row 2 and column 1.

It's now time for us to test our application. Just click on the Run button (▷), and you will see the form pop up, as shown below:

Click on the button labeled "Show Fruits". You will see the list of fruits displayed on the Excel sheet, as shown below:

	A	B	C	D
1	My Favorite Fruits			
2	Mango			
3	Banana			
4	Orange			
5	Others			
6				

Congratulations, that's how to use arrays in VBA!

Chapter 4- Operators in VBA

Operators are program elements that can be used either as a statement or as an expression. They are used when we need to manipulate data. A good example of an operator is the plus symbol (+), which is used whenever we need to sum up some numerical data. We can also use operators for the purpose of comparing data. A good example of such an operator is the less than symbol (<), which can be used when we need to compare two numbers.

VBA supports four types of operators, which include the following:

1.   Arithmetic operators- these are the operators that are used for the purpose of doing arithmetic operations like addition, multiplication, subtraction, division and others.

2.   Comparison operators- these are the types of operators used for comparison of values. They include the less than (<), equal to, greater than (>) and the not equal to (!=) operators.

3.   String operators- these are the operators used for manipulation of the string data.

4.   Logical operators- these are the operators used when we need to do a comparison of more than one condition.

Now we need to give an example demonstrating how these operators can be used in VBA. Open a blank Excel document and name it "VBA_Operator.xlsm". Ensure you save it as a Macro-Enabled Workbook, as shown below:

Click on the "Save" button to save it. On the Excel sheet, click on the "DEVELOPER" tab. Click on the dropdown for "Insert".

A list of elements will be shown in the drop down, so you just have to hover over them and you will see their respective names.

Our aim is to add a command button to the spreadsheet. Click on the CoomandButton control from the Insert dropdown (ActiveX Controls), then drag so as to draw it on the spreadsheet. Don't confuse the 'Choose the Button' element for a form.

We now need to change the properties of our button. Just right click on this button, then choose "Properties". You will see a new window pop up:

Properties

CommandB CommandBut ▾

Alphabetic	Categorized

(Name)	CommandButt
Accelerator	
AutoLoad	False
AutoSize	False ▾
BackColor	☐ &H800000(
BackStyle	1 - fmBackStyl
Caption	CommandButt
Enabled	True
Font	Calibri
ForeColor	■ &H800000
Height	29.25
Left	289.5
Locked	True
MouseIcon	(None)
MousePointer	0 - fmMousePo
Picture	(None)
PicturePosition	7 - fmPictureP
Placement	2
PrintObject	True
Shadow	False
TakeFocusOnCli	True
Top	90.75
Visible	True
Width	142.5
WordWrap	False

Set the Name of the button to "button1" and the caption to "Click Here!" You have now created your button. Once you're done with editing the above, just close the window.

Arithmetic Operators

You must be familiar with these. They include the addition (+), subtraction (-), multiplication (*), division (/), exponentiation (^) and modulus (mod).

We are going to use the button we created previously to demonstrate how this operators can be used. Right click on the button then choose "View Code". You will see a new window pop up with some code. Just add the following code to it so that you have the following:

Private Sub btn1_Click()
Dim a As Integer, b As Integer

   a = 5
   b = 8

MsgBox a + b, vbOKOnly, "Addition (+) Operator"
End Sub

Click on "Save" to save the changes and close the window with the code. I want to show you another way you can run your code. On the window for the Excel sheet, look for the "Design Mode" button on the toolbar. If you see the button with a green background, as shown below, then it's in an Active state and you cannot run your code from there.

If the button has a white background, then it's not in an active state, and you are able to run your code from there. Click on the button and you will see it change its background to the following:

Design
Mode

You can then click on the "Click Here" button and you will see the following result:

Now that we have done the addition operator, you can then play around with the code to use the other operators, such as multiplication, subtraction and others.

String Operators

String data is good for holding data that has characters, numbers, and symbols. The "March-2017" is an example of some string data.

The string operators help us manipulate string data. A good example of this is the concatenation operator (&), which can help us to join the values of two strings. Let's demonstrate this using an example.

Create a new workbook, then a button by following the steps we did previously. Change the name of the button to "conc" and set the caption to "Concatenate". Move to the source code of the button and then add the following code to it:

Private Sub conc_Click()

MsgBox "Nicholas" & "Samuel", vbOKOnly, "Concatenation Operator"

End Sub

Once you are done with editing the code, close down this window and move to the Excel sheet. Ensure that the button for Design Mode is not in its active state and then click on the button. The following result will be observed:

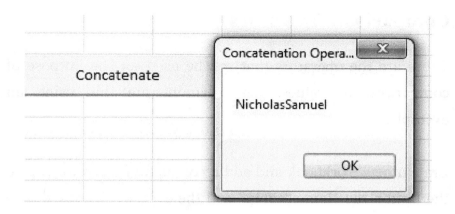

We have successfully used the concatenation operator (&)to link our two strings.

Comparison Operators

These are the operators that can be used for the purpose of comparison of values. Let's demonstrate this using an example.

Crate a new workbook and add a command button to it. Give the button the Name "comp" and the caption "Compare". Go to the source code for the button and add the following code to it:

```
Private Sub comp_Click()
    If 5 = 10 Then
        MsgBox "True", vbOKOnly, "Equal Operator"
    Else
        MsgBox "False", vbOKOnly, "Equal Operator"
    End If
End Sub
```

In this case, we are using the "If" statement to evaluate whether 5 and 10 are equal. The MsgBox is just an inbuilt method that displays a message box to us.

We have set the parameters "True" and "False" to be shown on our message box. The "vbOKOnly" options specify the kind of button that will be shown on the message box. The final option, which is "Equal Operator", represents the title to be used for the message box.

You can run the program and you will see the following output:

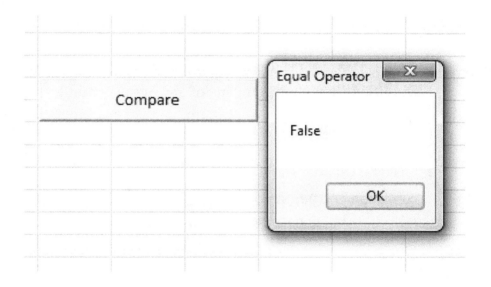

In this case, 5 and 10 are not equal, and that is why the result is "False", as shown above.

Logical Operators

These are used when we need to evaluate more than one condition. They include the following:

1.   AND- this is used for a combination of more than one condition. If all the conditions are true, this will evaluate to a true, while if any of these are false, this will evaluate to a false.

2.   OR- this is used for combining more than one condition. It evaluates to true of any of the conditions is true, and to false if all the conditions are false.

3.   NOT- this is similar to an inverse function. If a condition is true, the operator will return false, while if the condition is false, the operator will return a true.

Let's demonstrate how these operators can be used.
In your workbook, create three buttons.

For the first button, give it the name "buttonAND", with a caption of "AND Operator".

For the second button, give it the name "buttonOR" and a caption of "OR Operator".

For the third button, give it the name "buttonNOT" with a caption of "NOT Operator". Finally, you should have the GUI (Graphical User Interface) given below:

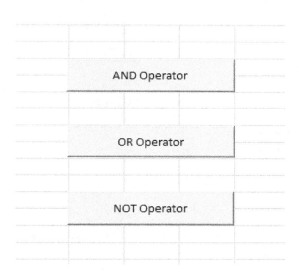

Right click on the button for "AND Operator", choose "View Code" then add the following code to it:

Private Sub buttonAND_Click()

  If (1 = 1) And (0 = 0) Then

      MsgBox "The result of AND operator is TRUE", vbOKOnly, "AND operator"

    Else

      MsgBox "The result of AND operator is FALSE", vbOKOnly, "AND operator"

End If

End Sub

In the statement "If (1 = 1) AND (0 = 0) Then", we are using the AND operator to compare two conditions, which include (1=1) and (0=0). If these two conditions evaluate to a true, the block of statement below "If" will be executed, and if false, the block of statement below "Else" will be executed.

Right click on the button for "OR Operator", choose "View Code" and add the code given below to it:

```
Private Sub buttonOR_Click()
    If (1 = 1) Or (5 = 0) Then
        MsgBox "The result of OR operator is TRUE", vbOKOnly, "OR operator"

    Else
        MsgBox "The result of OR operator is FALSE", vbOKOnly, "OR operator"

    End If
End Sub
```

In the "If (1 = 1) Or (5 = 0) Then" statement, we are using the OR operator to compare the conditions (1=1) and (5=0). If any of these conditions evaluates to a true, the statement below the "If" will be executed, while if both evaluate to a false, the statement below "Else" will be executed.

Right click on the button for "NOT Operator", and then add the code given below to it:

Private Sub buttonNOT_Click()
   If Not (0 = 0) Then
       MsgBox "The result of NOT operator is TRUE", vbOKOnly, "NOT operator"

      Else
       MsgBox "The result of NOT operator is FALSE", vbOKOnly, "NOT operator"

   End If
End Sub

In the "If Not (0 = 0) Then" statement, we are using the NOT operator to negate the result of (0=0). If the result is true, the statement below Else will be executed, while if true, the statement below If will be executed.

You can then close the window with the codes, go back to the Excel sheet with the buttons, de-activate the Design Mode button and try to click on each button. First, click on the "AND Operator" and you will see the following result:

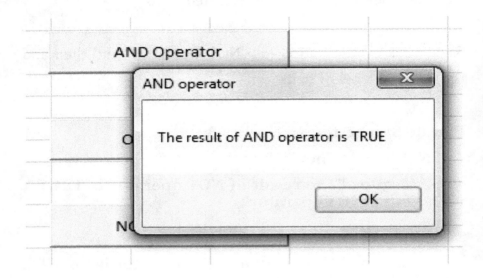

The reason is because the conditions 1=1 and 0=0 evaluated to a true. The result of the AND operator is also True.

Next, click the button for "OR Operator" and observe the result. It should be as follows:

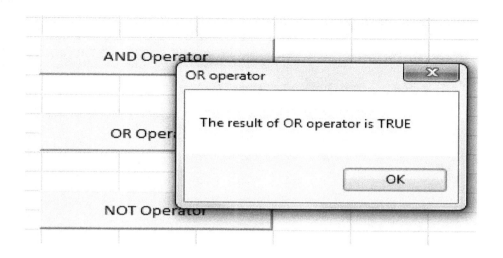

We were comparing the conditions 1=1 and 5=0. The first condition is true, hence the result of the OR operator is true.

Next, click the button for "NOT Operator" and observe the result. You should get the following:

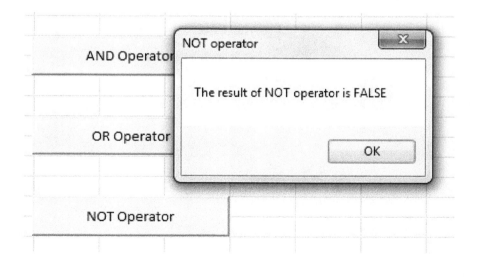

Of course, the result for the condition 0=0 is true, and when negated, we get a false. This explains the source of the above result.

Chapter 5- Functions and Subroutines

Subroutines

A subroutine is a block of code created to perform a specific task, but it doesn't return any result. Subroutines are used when we need to break down a large piece of code into small chunks that are easy to manage.

The following are the set of rules that you should adhere to when you are naming subroutines and functions:

- Don't use a space in naming a subroutine or a function.

- The name for the subroutine or the function has to begin with either a letter or an underscore. Don't use a number or special character.

- The name for the function or subroutine should not be a keyword. A keyword refers to a word with some special meaning in VBA. These include words such as Sub, Private, Function and others.

We need to create an example that demonstrates how a subroutine can be used in VBA.

Declaration of a subroutine should follow the syntax given below:

Private Sub yourSubRoutine(ByVal arg1 As String, ByVal arg2 As String)

  'add some code
End Sub

In the above case, we have used the "Sub" keyword to declare that we are creating a subroutine with the name "yourSubRoutine". Note that the "Private" keyword only specifies the scope for our subroutine.

We have then added arguments to this subroutine with the names "arg1" and "arg2", and both of these arguments are of String data type.

The statement "End Sub" helps us end the body of our subroutine.

Let's begin by creating the user interface for our example application, which will only have a command button.

Open a new Excel workbook and save its name as a macro-enabled workbook. Add a button by following our usual steps. Set the Name of the button to "buttonName" and the caption to "Name SubRoutine". You should finally have the interface given below:

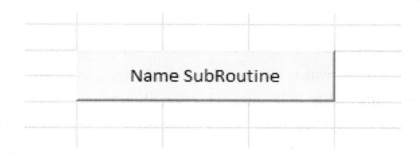

Now, it's time for you to add the subroutine. Just right click on the button, then choose "View Code". You will be taken to the code window, in which you should add the code given below:

Private Sub showName(ByVal firstName As String)
   MsgBox firstName
End Sub

In the above case, we have defined a subroutine named "showName". This subroutine is taking a single argument named "firstName", and this is a string argument. The MsgBox will have the value of the firstName, and we have then ended our subroutine.

We should then go ahead and create the code for the click event. The code for this should be as follows:

Private Sub buttonName_Click()
  showName "Nicholas"
End Sub

Remember we had declared the subroutine named "showName", which was to take a single argument. We have then called this subroutine in the showName "Nicholas" statement, and we have passed the value of the argument firstName as Nicholas. Your whole code window should now have the following code:

Private Sub showName(ByVal firstName As String)
  MsgBox firstName
End Sub

Private Sub buttonName_Click()
  showName "Nicholas"
End Sub

Now save your code and close the code window. It's time for us to test our app.

Just de-activate the Design Mode button and then try to run the app by clicking the "Name SubRoutine" button. You will see the result given below:

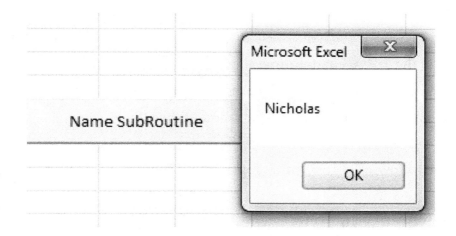

Functions

A function is simply a block of code for performing a specific task and then returning a result from this task. Functions are often used when you need to perform repetitive tasks. Note that the rules for defining subroutines and functions are the same in VBA, and the difference them is that a subroutine doesn't return results while a function does.

The following is the syntax for defining functions in VBA:

Private Function functionName(ByVal arg1 As Integer, ByVal arg2 As Integer)

   functionName = arg1 + arg2
End Function

In the above syntax, we have used the "Function" keyword to define a function name "functionName". This function is taking two arguments, namely arg1 and arg2, which are of an integer data type.

In the "functionName = arg1 + arg2" statement, we have added the values of arg1 and arg1 and the result has been assigned to the name of our function. Lastly, we have used the End keyword to end the function.

We want to demonstrate how functions can be used by creating an example app.

In the same workbook, add another button, and then change its properties. Give the name "buttonAdd" and set the caption to "Add Function". You should then end up with the interface given below:

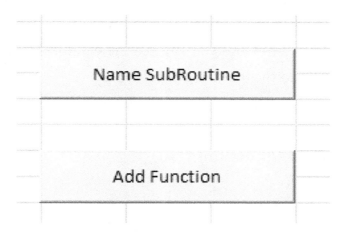

Now that the interface is ready, it's time for us to move to the code window and add the necessary code. Add the following code to create the function:

Private Function addFunction(ByVal number1 As Integer, ByVal number2 As Integer)

    addFunction = number1 + number2

End Function

We have created a function named "addFunction". This function is taking two integer arguments named "number1" and "number2". In the "addFunction = number1 + number2" statement, we have added the values of these two numbers and their result assigned to the name of our function, which is "addFunction". Lastly, we have ended our function.

It's now time for us to add the code that will help us handle the click event. Just right click on the "Add Function" button, choose "View Code" and you will see the window in which you can do this. Add the following code:

Private Sub buttonAdd_Click()
  MsgBox addFunction(5, 10)
End Sub

In the "MsgBox addFunction(5, 10)" statement, we are calling the "addFunction()" function and passing the values of the parameters to this function. The values are 5 and 10, which are to be added together. The whole code for this button should now be as follows:

Private Function addFunction(ByVal number1 As Integer, ByVal number2 As Integer)

  addFunction = number1 + number2

End Function

Private Sub buttonAdd_Click()

   MsgBox addFunction(5, 10)

End Sub

At this point, you can save your code and then return to the worksheet with the interface. Follow the usual steps to run the program. Once you click on the "Add Function" button, you will see the following result:

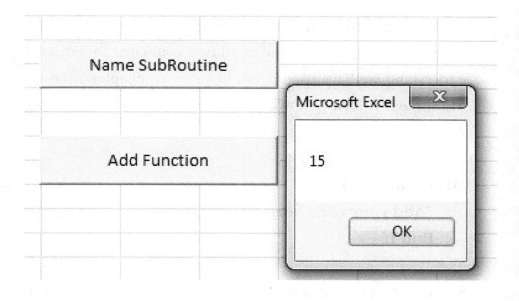

That's it! You have created both a function and a subroutine! We have just added the value of number1 and number2, hence the result is 15.

Chapter 6- Decision Making Statements and Loops in VBA

VBA supports the use of decision making statements. Let's discuss these in detail.

The "If" Statement

This statement takes a condition, and the code contained in it will only be executed if the condition evaluates to a true. I understand we have used it in our previous chapters, but we will discuss it further now. The statement takes the following syntax:

If condition Then
    'Add your code here
    End If

So far, we have not used an input dialog box. Suppose you want to find out the age of an individual. If they are under 18 years, you want to inform them that they are underage. Let's create a simple example that makes use of the If statement to achieve this.

Open a blank Excel worksheet. Save it as a macro-enabled workbook. Click the DEVELOPER tab from the toolbar and then click the "Visual Basic" button on the left of the toolbar. A new window will pop up.

You will be running your code from Sheet1. On the left window, right click the "Sheet1" option, then choose "View Code".

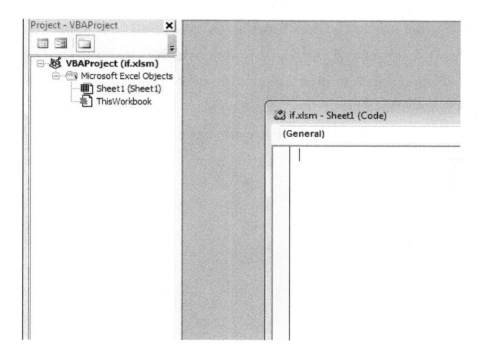

This is a window in which you can write and run your code from. Add the following code:

Function IF_Statement()

```
Dim Age As Integer

Age = InputBox("Enter your Age ", "Your Age")
    If Age < 18 Then
        MsgBox "You are underage!"
    End If
End Function
```

In this case, we have created a function named "IF_Statement()". This function is taking no argument. We have then defined the variable Age, which is an integer. This age should be obtained from an input box, hence we have used the InputBox() function. The statement "If Age < 18 then" will help you evaluate the value of the age and if it evaluates to a true, the statement below it will be executed. Run the program then enter a value for age:

After entering your age, click the "OK" button and observe what happens next. You should see the following message box:

That is how an If statement can be used in VBA.

If Else Statement

Sometimes, you may want to do something if a condition is true and something else if the condition is false. This is a good application of the If Else statement. The statement takes the following syntax:

If condition Then
    code
  Else
    other code
  End If

Suppose you want to get the username and the password for a user via an input box. If the credentials match, you welcome them, but if they don't match, you alert them that they have been denied access. This can be done by use of the "If...Else" statement, as shown below:

Function IF_Else_Statement()
  Dim Username As String
  Dim Password As String

  Username = InputBox("Enter your Username ", "Your Username")

```
    Password = InputBox("Enter your Password ",
"Your Password")

    If Username = "Nicholas" And Password =
"1234" Then
        MsgBox "Welcome Nicholas!"
    Else
        MsgBox "Access is denied"
    End If
End Function
```

Try to run the above code, then enter the username and password as "Nicholas" and "1234" respectively. You will get the following message box:

Try to enter a wrong credential, either in the name or the password, and you will see the following message box:

Note that the value of Username was set to Nicholas, while the value for password was set to 1234. If a mismatch occurs, the statement below the Else part is to be executed as demonstrated above!

Loops

Loops help us to do tasks repetitively. In VBA, a loop can help you to loop through a number of cells using just few lines of code. Let's discuss how some of the VBA loops can help you achieve this.

Single Loop

This loop is good for when you need to loop through the Excel cells in a one-dimensional manner. Let's demonstrate this using an example.

Add a button to your workbook, with the caption set to "Populate Cells" and the name set to "loopButton". You should end up with the following:

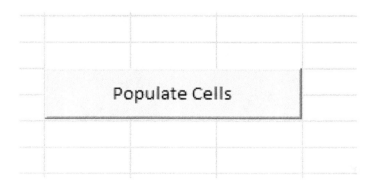

You can then right click the button and choose "View Code" to add a click event to the button. Add the following code:

```
Private Sub buttonLoop_Click()
Dim x As Integer

For x = 1 To 10
    Cells(x, 1).Value = "Nicholas"
Next x
End Sub
```

Save the file and try to run it by clicking the "Populate Cells" button. You will observe the following in your Excel sheet:

	A	B	C	D	E	F	G	H
1	Nicholas							
2	Nicholas							
3	Nicholas							
4	Nicholas				Populate Cells			
5	Nicholas							
6	Nicholas							
7	Nicholas							
8	Nicholas							
9	Nicholas							
10	Nicholas							
11								

The cells A1 to A10 have been populated with the value you specified. The code between the For and Next keywords was executed 10 times. When the value of x=1, the value "Nicholas" was entered at the cell that is at the intersection of row 1 and column 1. When x=2, the value "Nicholas" is entered to the cell at the intersection of row 2 and column 1.

Double Loop

This is a good loop when you need to work on Excel cells in a two-dimensional manner. Let's demonstrate with an example.

Add a command button to your Excel worksheet. Give it the Name "btnLoop" and a caption of "Two-Dimensional Population". You should end up with the following interface:

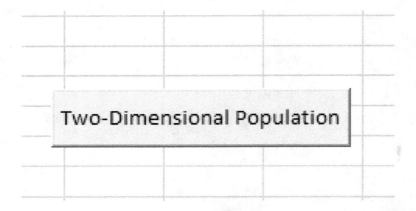

Add the following button click code to the button:

```
Private Sub btnLoop_Click()
Dim x As Integer, y As Integer

For x = 1 To 10
   For y = 1 To 2
      Cells(x, y).Value = "Nicholas"
```

Next y

Next x

End Sub

Save the code and then run the app by clicking on your button. The cells will be populated as shown below:

	A	B	C	D	E	F	G	H
1	Nicholas	Nicholas						
2	Nicholas	Nicholas						
3	Nicholas	Nicholas						
4	Nicholas	Nicholas						
5	Nicholas	Nicholas						
6	Nicholas	Nicholas				Two-Dimensional Population		
7	Nicholas	Nicholas						
8	Nicholas	Nicholas						
9	Nicholas	Nicholas						
10	Nicholas	Nicholas						

When x=1 and y=1, the value "Nicholas" will be entered in the cell at the intersection of row 1 and column 1. After reaching "Next y", the value of y will be increased and the VBA will move back to the "For y..." statement. You will have x=1 and y=2 and the value "Nicholas" will be entered at the intersection of row 1 and column 2. The next y is ignored, as the value of y ranges between 1 and 2. After reaching "Next x", VBA will increase x by 1, so you have x=2 and y=1. The value "Nicholas" is then entered at the intersection of row 2 and column 1.

Triple Loop

This loop is useful when one needs to loop over two-dimensional cells in a number of sheets. To demonstrate this, add a command button to your worksheet with the name "trippleButton" and the caption of "Triple Loop".
You should have the following interface:

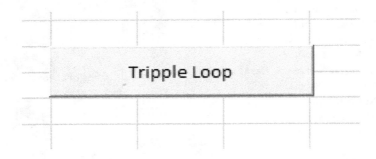

Add the following code to the button:

```
Private Sub trippleButton_Click()
Dim b As Integer, x As Integer, y As Integer

For b = 1 To 3
   For x = 1 To 6
     For y = 1 To 2
        Worksheets(b).Cells(x, y).Value = "Nicholas"
     Next y
   Next x
```

Next b

End Sub

Run the code and see the result. It will populate the cells with the value "Nicholas".

Chapter 7- User Forms in VBA

A user form is a dialog box that allows the users to enter data.

We will show you how you can create your own form in VBA and use it to populate data in an Excel sheet.

Begin by creating a new workspace. Open the VBA window by clicking on Visual Basic from the DEVELOPER tab. On this new window, click on "Insert" from the toolbar then choose User Form". You should get the following:

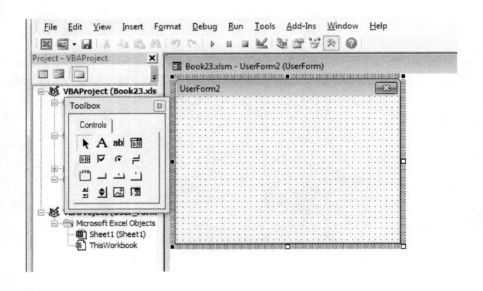

The "Toolbox" window has all the controls that you need to design your form. We need to create a user form that looks like the following:

Below is a description of the name and caption for each element used in the above form:

1. Student Reg. Number Label Box. Name-studentRegL, caption-Student Reg. Number
2. First Name Label Box. Name-fNameL, caption-First Name
3. Last Name Label Box. Name-lNameL, caption-Last Name

4. Date of Birth Label Box. Name-dobL, caption- Date of Birth

5. Gender Label Box. Name-genderL, caption-Gender

6. Course Label Box. Name-courseL, caption-Course

7. Submit Button. Name- btnSubmit, caption- Submit

8. Cancel Button. Name- btnCancel, caption- Cancel.

9. Student Reg. Number Text Box, Name-studentRegT

10. First Name Text Box. Name-fNameT

11. Last Name Text Box. Name- lNameT

12. Male Radio Button- radioMale, caption- Male

13. Female Radio Button- radioFemale, caption- Female

14. Date Combo Box- Name-cmbDate

15. Month Combo Box. Name-cmbMonth

16. Year Combo Box. Name-cmbYear

17. Course Text Box. Name- txtCourse

Note that where you don't see the caption, it is not applicable. To change these, you just have click on the element, right click on it and then choose "Properties". You will see the window for changing these properties on the bottom left of the screen.

Now, on that form, right click on it then choose "View Code". You will see a new form. In the drop downs located at the top of the form, choose "Userform" on the left and "Initialize" on the right.

You should then add the following code below the sub-procedure:

```
Private Sub UserForm_Initialize()
 'Empty Student Reg Number Text box and Set the Cursor
   studentRegT.Value = ""
   studentRegT.SetFocus

   'Empty all text box fields
   fNameT.Value = ""
   lNameT.Value = ""

   'Clear All fields related to Date of Birth
   cmbDate.Clear
   cmbMonth.Clear
   cmbYear.Clear

   'Fill the Date Drop Down box
   With cmbDate
     .AddItem "1"
     .AddItem "2"
     .AddItem "3"
```

```
.AddItem "4"
.AddItem "5"
.AddItem "6"
.AddItem "7"
.AddItem "8"
.AddItem "9"
.AddItem "10"
.AddItem "11"
.AddItem "12"
.AddItem "13"
.AddItem "14"
.AddItem "15"
.AddItem "16"
.AddItem "17"
.AddItem "18"
.AddItem "19"
.AddItem "20"
.AddItem "21"
.AddItem "22"
.AddItem "23"
.AddItem "24"
.AddItem "25"
.AddItem "26"
.AddItem "27"
.AddItem "28"
.AddItem "29"
```

```vb
    .AddItem "30"
    .AddItem "31"
End With

'Fill the Month Drop Down box
With cmbMonth
    .AddItem "JAN"
    .AddItem "FEB"
    .AddItem "MAR"
    .AddItem "APR"
    .AddItem "MAY"
    .AddItem "JUN"
    .AddItem "JUL"
    .AddItem "AUG"
    .AddItem "SEP"
    .AddItem "OCT"
    .AddItem "NOV"
    .AddItem "DEC"
End With

'Fill the Year Drop Down box
With cmbYear
    .AddItem "1980"
    .AddItem "1981"
    .AddItem "1982"
    .AddItem "1983"
```

```
.AddItem "1984"
.AddItem "1985"
.AddItem "1986"
.AddItem "1987"
.AddItem "1988"
.AddItem "1989"
.AddItem "1990"
.AddItem "1991"
.AddItem "1992"
.AddItem "1993"
.AddItem "1994"
.AddItem "1995"
.AddItem "1996"
.AddItem "1997"
.AddItem "1998"
.AddItem "1999"
.AddItem "2000"
.AddItem "2001"
.AddItem "2002"
.AddItem "2003"
.AddItem "2004"
.AddItem "2005"
.AddItem "2006"
.AddItem "2007"
.AddItem "2008"
.AddItem "2009"
```

```vba
        .AddItem "2010"
        .AddItem "2011"
        .AddItem "2012"
        .AddItem "2013"
        .AddItem "2014"
        .AddItem "2015"
        .AddItem "2016"
        .AddItem "2017"


    End With


    'Reset the Radio Button. Set to False once the form has loaded.
    radioyes.Value = False
    radiono.Value = False
End Sub
```

The comments in the code should help you understand the purpose of the different sections of code. The comments begin with a single quote.

Now, it's time for us to add a click event to our submit button. We need it to be made in such a way that after it is clicked, the details will be entered into an Excel sheet. Just right click on the button and then choose "View Code". Add the following code to this button:

```
Private Sub btnSubmit_Click()
Dim emptyRow As Long

    'activate Sheet1
    Sheet1.Activate

    'Determine the emptyRow
    emptyRow                                              =
WorksheetFunction.CountA(Range("A:A")) + 1

    'Transfer the information
    Cells(emptyRow, 1).Value = studentRegT.Value
    Cells(emptyRow, 2).Value = fNameT.Value
    Cells(emptyRow, 3).Value = lNameT.Value
    Cells(emptyRow, 4).Value = cmbDate.Value & "/" &
cmbMonth.Value & "/" & cmbYear.Value


    If radioMale.Value = True Then
        Cells(emptyRow, 6).Value = "Male"
```

Else

   Cells(emptyRow, 6).Value = "Female"

End If

   Cells(emptyRow, 7).Value = courseT.Value

End Sub

Note that we are adding the form details to Sheet1, so we had to begin by activating it. The values for the Date of birth have to be joined to get a single date.

Next, we need to add the code for the cancel button. When this button is clicked, it should close the form. Add the following code to it:

Private Sub btnCancel_Click()

 Unload Me

End Sub

The "Unload Me" statement will close the form once the button is closed.

It's now time for us to load the form and test it. Just save what you have done and click on the Run icon. You should see the form pop up. Enter the details for the student and then click on the "Submit" button. These details should be added to the Excel sheet. This is demonstrated below:

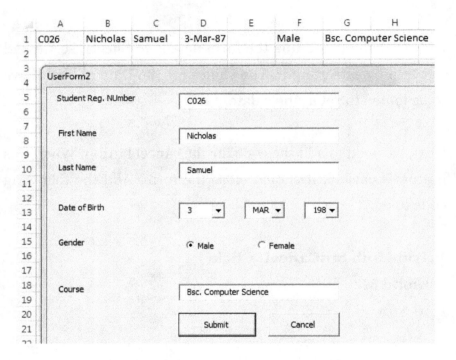

That's it! Your form is now working! We used an If statement in the field for Gender, so that if you don't choose, Female will be used as the default one. You also have to specify the cells in which the values from different fields will be populated. Again, run the form and then click on the "Cancel" button. You will note that it will be closed.

Chapter 8- Working with Text Files

In VBA, it is possible to read the contents of an Excel sheet then write the read contents into a text file. There are two ways you can implement this:

1. Using File System Object
2. Using Write Command

The File System Object (FSO)

This tool helps VBA developers to work with folders, drivers and files. The following are the objects that are supported:

1. Drive- this is an object. It has methods and properties that will allow one to gather the information regarding a drive that has been attached to the system.

2. File- it is an object. It has the methods and properties that will allow the developers to create, move and delete a file.

3. Drives- this is a collection. It will give you the list of the drives that have been attached to the system, either logically or physically.

4. Files- this is a collection. It will provide you with a list of all files that are contained in a folder.

5. TextStream- this is an object. It will help the developer to read then write to text files.

6. Folder- this is an object that makes it possible for the developer to create, move and delete a folder.

7. Folders- this is a collection that will give you a list of all the folders that are contained in a particular folder.

Let's discuss the drive.

This object can help you find out the properties of some disk. You can use it to find out the drive letter, the available space, file system, volume size and other details. The following are the properties that are supported by this object:

- AvailableSpace

- DriveType

- ShareName

- FreeSpace

- IsReady

- DriveLetter

- Path

- SerialNumber

- FileSystem

- TotalSize

- RootFolder

- VolumeName

Let's use an example to demonstrate how you can use the FSO object.

The first step should be enabling Microsoft Scripting Runtime. This can be done by following the steps given below:

Open the VBA editor, click on "Tools", and then choose "References" from the toolbar.

Check the box for "Microsoft Scripting Runtime", and then click "Ok".

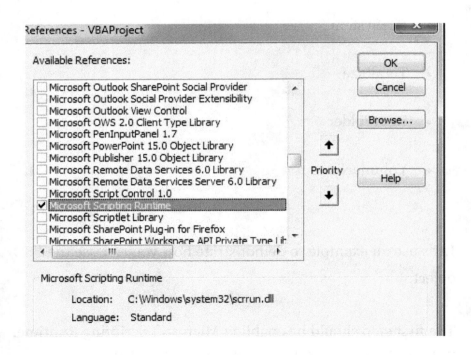

You've done it. Now, in your Excel sheet, add the data that you want to write to the text file. Next, add a command button to this sheet. In my case, I have the following:

	A	B	C	D	E	F	G	H	I
1	C026	Nicholas	Samuel	3-Mar-87		Male	Bsc. Computer Science		
2	C027	John	Kariuki	4-Apr-86		Male	Bsc. Information Technology		
3	E019	Mercy	Mumo	4-May-87		Female	Bsc. Electrical Engineering		
4	E019	John	Bosco	6-Oct-92		Male	Bsc. Acturial Science		
5									
6						Populate Text File			
7									
8									

Now, it's time for us to add the code for the click event so that, after clicking the command button, the text file will be populated. Add the following code to the button:

Private Sub writetxtfile_Click()
   Dim FilePath As String
   Dim CellData As String
   Dim LastColumn As Long
   Dim LastRow As Long

   Dim fso As FileSystemObject
   Set fso = New FileSystemObject
   Dim stream As TextStream

```vba
    LastColumn                                    =
ActiveSheet.UsedRange.Columns.Count
    LastRow = ActiveSheet.UsedRange.Rows.Count


    'Create the TextStream.


    Set    stream    =    fso.OpenTextFile("F:\myfile.log",
ForWriting, True)

    CellData = ""

    For x = 1 To LastRow
      For y = 1 To LastColumn
        CellData = Trim(ActiveCell(x, y).Value)
        stream.WriteLine "The located at (" & x & "," & y
& ")" & CellData

      Next y
    Next x


    stream.Close
    MsgBox ("The writing was successful")
End Sub
```

Note that we have defined two string variables, two long variables, one variable of type File System Object and one TextStream variable. The path to which the text file will be created and the location of each Excel cell have been defined as a string.

In the "Set stream = fso.OpenTextFile("F:\myfile.log", ForWriting, True)", statement, we are setting the location of the new file (myfile) in our computer. Ensure that you specify the right location based on where you want it stored. The x and y variables help us iterate through the values that are contained in the Excel sheet.

You can then follow the usual steps to run the program. Click the command button and you will get the following message box:

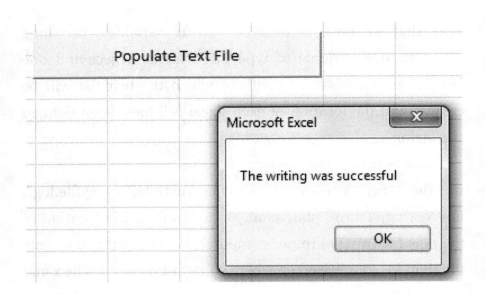

You can then navigate to the directory you had specified to store the file and it will have been created with your Excel contents.

Using Write Command

With this tool, there is no need to add references, but it will be impossible to work with files, drives and folders. However, with this tool, it is possible to write a text stream into a text file. Let's use an example to demonstrate how this command works. In the same workbook, add a second command button. In my case, I have the following:

	A	B	C	D	E	F
1	C026	Nicholas	Samuel	3-Mar-87		Male
2	C027	John	Kariuki	4-Apr-86		Male
3	E019	Mercy	Mumo	4-May-87		Female
4	E019	John	Bosco	6-Oct-92		Male
5						
6				Write Command		
7						
8						
9				Populate Text File		
10						
11						

Note that I have just added the "Write Command" button. The following should be the code for the button:

Private Sub writeComm_Click()
  Dim FilePath As String
  Dim CellData As String
  Dim LastColumn As Long

```vba
Dim LastRow As Long

LastColumn                                          =
ActiveSheet.UsedRange.Columns.Count
  LastRow = ActiveSheet.UsedRange.Rows.Count

FilePath = "F:\myfile2.txt"
Open FilePath For Output As #2

CellData = ""
For x = 1 To LastRow
  For y = 1 To LastColumn
    CellData = "The Value at location (" & x & "," & y
& ")" & Trim(ActiveCell(x, y).Value)

    Write #2, CellData
  Next y
Next x

Close #2
MsgBox ("The writing was successful")
End Sub
```

Run the script and you will find myfile2 created in the
directory you have specified. The variable x helps us iterate
through the rows of the sheet, while the y helps us iterate
through the columns of the sheet.

Chapter 9- Creating Charts

It is possible to create or generate charts in VBA from your own data. This is useful for any VBA developer. Suppose you have the following data for a school in your Excel sheet:

	A	B	C
1	Year	Number of Students	
2	2013	2000	
3	2014	1800	
4	2015	2800	
5	2016	3200	
6			

We want to create a code that will help us generate a bar chart from the above data.

Add a command button to the worksheet as shown below:

	A	B	C	D
1	Year	Number of Students		
2	2013	2000		
3	2014	1800		
4	2015	2800		
5	2016	3200		
6				
7	Create Bar Chart			
8				
9				

After that, add the following code to the click event for the button:

```
Private Sub chartButton_Click()
  Dim barChart As Chart
  'Create your new chart.
  Set barChart = Charts.Add
  With barChart
    .Name = "School Population"
    .ChartType = xlColumnClustered
    'Link chart to source of data.
    .SetSourceData
Source:=Sheets("Sheet1").Range("A2:B5"), _
    PlotBy:=xlRows
    .HasTitle = True
```

```
.ChartTitle.Text = "=Sheet1!R1C2"

.Axes(xlCategory, xlPrimary).HasTitle = True

.Axes(xlCategory,
xlPrimary).AxisTitle.Characters.Text = "Year"

.Axes(xlValue, xlPrimary).HasTitle = True

.Axes(xlValue,
xlPrimary).AxisTitle.Characters.Text = "Student
Population"

   End With
End Sub
```

The main logic has been achieved in the "Set barChart = Charts.Add" statement. This is the statement that helps to create the chart, and it is associated to the "barChart" variable that we had created. Notice the use of ".HasTitle = True" property, which helps us to turn on the title for the chart. The property ".ChartTitle.Text" helps you to set the text you need to appear at the top of your chart. The "Axes" method helps us add some text below both the X and Y axis.

The .Axes(xlCategory, xlPrimary).AxisTitle.Characters.Text = "Year" statement helps us to set text for the X axis.

The .Axes(xlValue, xlPrimary).AxisTitle.Characters.Text = "Student Population" statement helps us to set the text for the Y axis.

In the "Axis" method, you need two things, the Type and the Axis Group. The type, in this case, can be xlValue, xlCategory, or xlSeriesAxis, which is used in 3D charts.

Run the program and you will get the bar chart given below:

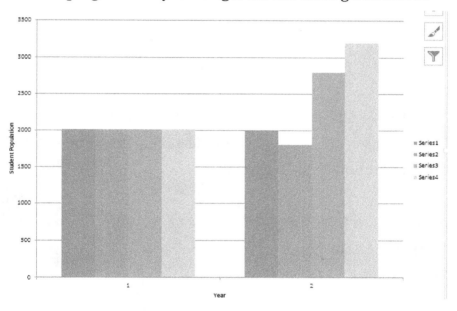

You have generated your bar chart! The values for the first column of your data have been grouped into one, while those for the second column into the other. To match these, you only have to consider their colors.

We can use the same data to create a line graph as well. Add another button to the worksheet:

	A	B	C	D	E	F
1	Year	Number				
2	2013	4000				
3	2014	1800				
4	2015	2800				
5	2016	500				
6						
7						
8	Create Line Graph			Create Bar Chart		
9						

Note I have added the button for "Create Line Graph" and I have changed the data so as to reflect a greater variance. The code for button should be as follows:

```
Private Sub lineBtn_Click()
Dim rng As Range
Dim linecht As Object

'The data range for your chart
  Set rng = ActiveSheet.Range("A2:B5")

'Create new chart
  Set linecht = ActiveSheet.Shapes.AddChart2

'Add some data to the chart
  linecht.Chart.SetSourceData Source:=rng
```

'Determine the type of the chart
 linecht.Chart.ChartType = xlXYScatterLines
End Sub

In the above code, the main logic is in the Set linecht = ActiveSheet.Shapes.AddChart2 statement, as this is where the chart is being created. In our previous example, a new tab was created for the bar chart. In this case, we want to do it in the active same tab or page, as the use of the ActiveSheet method.

The Range () function has helped us specify the cells with the values to be used for creating the chart. The "ChartType" function has helped us specify the kind of chart for us to create. The code should generate the following chart:

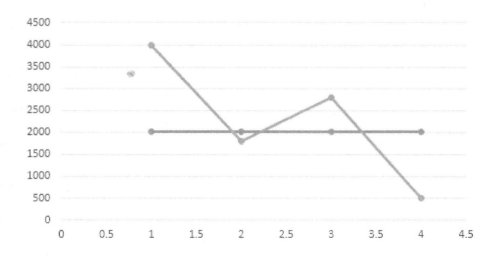

Play around with the chart by adding values on the axis and the title of the chart.

Chapter 10- VBA Events

In VBA, events make your work easier. The events are triggered by actions such as a manual change in cell value. Anytime you open, close and save a workbook, print out something, type, click on some cell, double-click or right-click, an event will have happened, and it is possible for you to accomplish these tasks via a code that you have written.

Suppose you expect someone else to use your workbook and you need to make it so that once they have opened it, they will be taken to the correct sheet. This can be handled using an event-handling macro given below:

Private Sub Workbook_Open()

'go to right worksheet on opening

Worksheets("ImportantSheet").Select

End Sub

The Event-handling Macro

You should determine whether the macro is expecting an event for the entire workbook or just a single worksheet. Examples of events that can be done on a workbook include opening, closing, saving a file, and printing anything. Events that can be applied to a worksheet include a click on a cell, changing a cell value and right-clicking a cell.

On the VBA editor, double click on the workbook or just right click it and choose "View Code".

After that, choose "Workbook" from the dropdown with General to attach the code to the workbook:

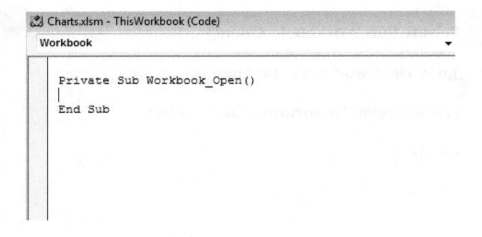

The dropdown on the right side will help you choose the event that you will need to handle.

However, in this case, you may not have to choose, as it may be selected automatically for you. The code that you expect to run after the user has opened the workbook can be added.

Canceling Events

Whenever you see that an event begins with "Before", it is an indication that it is possible for you to react to the event that is to occur and bar it from occurring if you want to do so. In the example given below, we will be preventing anyone from closing the workbooks if the version control number has not been filled:

```
Option Explicit

'to hold the current version number

Private VersionNumber As Integer

Private Sub Workbook_Open()

'read version number in the cell A1

Worksheets(1).Select

VersionNumber = Range("A1").Value

End Sub

Private Sub Workbook_BeforeSave(ByVal SaveAsUI As Boolean, Cancel As Boolean)


Dim NewVersionNumber As Integer
```

```vba
'if the version number has not been changed, cannot
close

Worksheets(1).Select

NewVersionNumber = Range("A1").Value

If VersionNumber = NewVersionNumber Then

'the user has not changed the version number, so
abort

MsgBox "The version number must be updated first"

Cancel = True

End If

End Sub
```

With the above code, once the user has opened the workbook, the value contained in the cell A1 will be read by the code you have attached to the Open. The value of this cell will then be stored in a variable named VersionNumber.

If someone tries to save the work, then the code for BeforeSave event will check to see whether this number has been updated. If this is not the case, the message specified in the MsgBox will be displayed and the event will be canceled. In the code, the section

'cancel this event

Cancel = True

is responsible for canceling the event that triggered the macro.

Workbook Events

The following steps can help you create a workbook event in VBA:

1. Identify the file you need to attach the code to, and then click on its "ThisWorkbook". You can also right click on "ThisWorkbook", and then choose "View Code.

2. On the dropdown with General, click on choose "Workbook".

3. Move to the dropdown located on the right side then select the event you need to attach the code.

The following are some of the more common workbook events:

1. BeforeClose- prevents a workbook from being closed if a specified

   condition is not true.

2. BeforePrint- prevents the user from printing if data has not been filled.

3. BeforeSave- this prevents the user from saving an incomplete workbook.

4. NewSheet- this will react to a user who is inserting a new workbook.

5. SheetCalculate- this will run once the user has pressed the F9 key so as to calculate the worksheet.

Let's give some examples of macros that you may be helpful for you to write.

Prevent Printing

Suppose you want to prevent the users from printing the workbook on Tuesdays. You just have to double click on the "ThisWorkbook" of the worksheet, choose "Workbook" on the left dropdown and "BeforePrint" on the right.

Workbook	▾	BeforePrint

The following code will then help you prevent the user from printing on Tuesdays and display a message:

```vba
Private Sub Workbook_BeforePrint(Cancel As Boolean)
If Weekday(Date) = vbTuesday Then

'bar printing on Tuesdays

MsgBox "Sorry, you can't use the printer on Tuesdays!"
Cancel = True

End If
End Sub
```

Note we have used the If statement of "If Weekday (Date) = vbTuesday" Then to to determine the date of the week. If it is on Tuesday, then the message for the MsgBox will be displayed, and no printing will happen.

Show a Message when opening New Sheet

It is impossible to prevent a user from creating a new sheet directly. However, you can respond to such an action then delete the sheet quietly. Let's demonstrate how to do this:

Open "ThisWorkbook", then choose "Workbook" on the left dropdown and "NewSheet" on the right dropdown.

Workbook	▾ NewSheet

Add the following code:

Private Sub Workbook_NewSheet(ByVal Sh As Object)
'The user has inserted some new worksheet. Delete it quietly

Application.DisplayAlerts = False

Sh.Delete

Application.DisplayAlerts = True

'Give the reason for deleting the worksheet

MsgBox "Sorry, the workbook is full"
End Sub

In this code, the "Sh" has been used to represent the new sheet the user has created. Appending the "Delete" function to this will cause it to be deleted.

Those are some of the events that can be handled at workbook level. Let's now discuss the events that can be handled at worksheet level.

Worksheet Events

The process of attaching events to worksheets is similar to the process of attaching events to workbooks. The following steps will help you achieve this:

1. Identify the worksheet you need, then double click on it. These are named in the order of Sheet1, Sheet2 ...

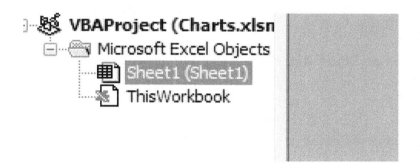

2. On the left dropdown with General, choose "Worksheet". This should be the only option that is provided to you.

3. On the right dropdown, select the event that you need to attach the code to.

Below are some of the available worksheet events:

1. Change- this event will be triggered once you have changed the value of a cell.

2. SelectionChange- this will run once you have selected a different cell or cells.

3. BeforeDoubleClick- this will be triggered once you have clicked the center of a cell but not on its edge.

4. BeforeRightClick- this is triggered once you have right clicked at the center of the cell, but not on the edge.

Let's now discuss how the macros for these events can be created.

Prevent Selection of a Cell

Sometimes you may need to react to the user once they have clicked on a particular cell. We can achieve this by using the "SelectionChange" event.

Our aim is to prevent the user from clicking on the above selected cell, which is B3. You should use the "SelectionChange" event then add the following code to it:

Private Sub Worksheet_SelectionChange(ByVal Target As Range)

'if the selected cell is not B3, it is fine

If Intersect(Target, Range("B3")) Is Nothing Then Exit Sub

'otherwise, the worksheet should be deleted

Cells.Clear

MsgBox "I had warned you!"
End Sub

You can save the above micro and then test it by clicking on the cell B3. Ensure that the Design Mode button has been deactivated before clicking on this. You should get the following message:

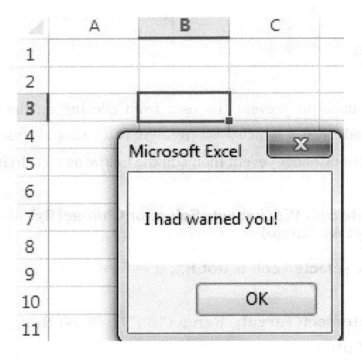

And the cells in the worksheet will be erased.

Reacting to Change in Cell Value

You may need to do something once the value of a particular cell has been changed by the user. In this case, we will use the "Change" event, so on the right dropdown, choose "Change" event. In our case, we will be preventing the user from typing an odd number into the cell. The following code will help you achieve this:

```
Private Sub Worksheet_Change(ByVal Target As Range)
'if it is single cell, and it is B3

If Target.Cells.Count = 1 Then

If Target.Row = 2 And Target.Column = 3 Then

'no odd number is allowed

If Target.Value Mod 2 = 1 Then

MsgBox "Odd numbers are not allowed"

Range("c2").Value = Target.Previous.Value
```

End If

End If

End If
End Sub

In this case, we are checking if the user has changed the value contained in the cell at row 2 and column 3. Save the code, and then type an odd number such as 7 in cell C2. You will see the following:

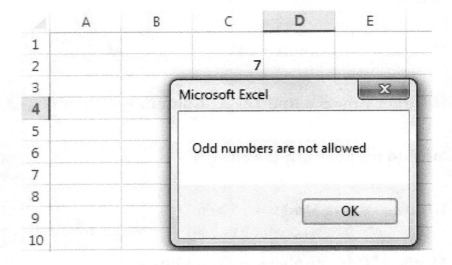

The statement "If Target.Value Mod 2 = 1 Then" helps us check whether the number is odd or not. The Mod operator returns remainder after division. If the remainder is 1 after dividing by 2, the number will be odd, and you will get the warning!

Chapter 11- Error Handling in VBA

Whenever your VBA app is running, there is a possibility that an error (is) will occur. Such errors might be brought about by a missing file, a missing database etc.

If you suspect that there is a possibility of an error occurring in a particular section, it will be a good idea to create some code that will be responsible for handling this error. Before this we do this, you should know the types of errors that can occur in VBA:

1. Syntax

2. Compilation

3. Runtime

Syntax Errors

These errors are very common, and if you have been doing VBA for while, you will have encountered them. Whenever you have typed a statement and you press the Enter key, the syntax will be analyzed and if it is wrong, you will be alerted to a syntax error.

A good example of this is when you use the If statement without the Then keyword. This will give you the following error message:

```
Private Sub Worksheet_Change(ByVal Target As Rang
If Target.Value Mod 2 = 1

End Sub
```

The following are some of the syntax errors that might occur:

' then has not been used
If x > y

' equals has not been added after i
For i 1 To 5
' right parenthesis are missing
y = left("ABCD",1

Note that syntax errors will only occur if something is missing in a single line. You might be interested in turning off the error dialog for the syntax errors. To do this, navigate through Tools->Options and check off the button for "Auto Syntax Check". If you have a syntax error in a line, it will remain red, but you will not see the dialog for syntax error.

Compilation Errors

These errors may occur in more than one line. The following are some of the examples that might cause a compilation error:

1. A For without Next

2. If without End If statement

3. A call to a Function or Sub which non-existent.

4. Passing wrong parameters to a Function or Sub.

5. Giving a Function or a Sub same name as a Module.

6. Variables not declared.

Consider the code given below:

```
Private Sub Forloop()
Dim x As Integer

For x = 1 To 10
    Cells(x, 1).Value = "Nicholas"
End Sub
```

In the above case, there is no "Next" to match the "For", so we will get the following error:

To find the compilation errors in your program, you should navigate through **"Debug->Compile VBA Project", which can be accessed from the Visual Basic menu.**

The first error encountered will be selected, so you can solve it. After that, run the VBA and the next error will be located. This will also locate the syntax found in your program.

Runtime Errors

These are the errors that occur as the application is running. A good example of this is when you are reading from an external workbook. If this is deleted, then you will get a runtime error.

Sometimes, you may suspect that a runtime error may occur. In such a case, you can write some code to handle it.

We need to demonstrate this by using a code to open a file. First, we will check if the file exists. If it is not found, a message will be shown and the VBA will exit the subroutine. You can just create a new button, then add the following code to it:

```
Private Sub fileCheck_Click()
    Dim myFile As String
    myFile = "F:\data.xlsx"

    ' Use Dir function to check for the file existence
    If Dir(myFile) = "" Then
        ' if the file is not found, display this message
        MsgBox "The file was not found " & myFile
        Exit Sub
    End If
```

```vba
    ' This code will only be excuted if the file is found
    Workbooks.Open myFile

End Sub
```

In this case, the variable "myFile" has been used to represent the location of the file. You have to set the correct location for the file in your system. We have passed this variable to the Dir() method, and if the file is not found, that is, "", the message for MsgBox will be shown. In this case, the "Exit Sub" statement will be executed and the subprocedure will no longer be executed. However, if the file is found, the "Workbooks.Open myFile" statement will be executed and the file will be opened.

In my case, I don't have the file "data.xlsl" as specified in the line "F:\data.xlsx". When I click the button, I get the following:

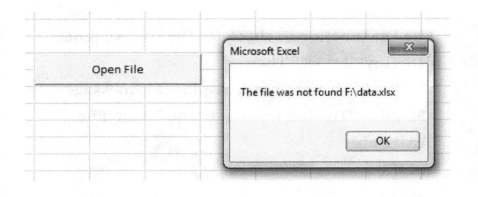

However, when I change the name of the file to "F:/charts.xlsm", which does exist, the new workbook is opened!

"On Error" Statement

This statement is used for handling errors. It usually does an action once an error has occurred during runtime. Below are the ways to use this error statement:

1. On Error Goto 0- the VBA will stop at the line with the error, and the error message will be shown.

2. On Error Resume Next- VBA will move to next line without showing an error message.

3. On Error Goto [label]- the VBA will move to a specified line or label without showing any error message.

4. On Error Goto -1- with this, the error will be cleared.

On Error Goto 0

This forms the default behavior for the VBA. It causes the VBA to stop at the line with the error then display an error message. Consider the code given below:

Dim x As Long, y As Long

```
x = 1
y = 1 / 0
x = 1
```

In this case, we have not used any On Error statements, so we expect the On Error Goto 0 to be used by default. Running the program gives the following error dialog:

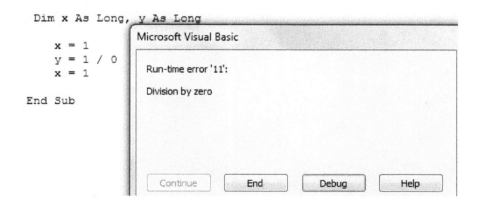

You can select either End or Debug. Choosing debug will cause the VBA to stop and highlight the line with the error, as shown below:

```
   Dim x As Long, y As Long

        x = 1
        y = 1 / 0
        x = 1

   End Sub
```

This is the best behavior for a developer who is writing their code, but is not so great when the application has been delivered to the users. This is due to the nature of the message, as the user may fail to understand the meaning.

On Error Goto [label]

This can be equated to the try and catch block used in languages such as C# and Java. Once the error has occurred, it will be sent to a specific label, which is below the sub. Consider the example given below:

Private Sub errorCheck()
   On Error GoTo last

   Dim x As Long, y As Long

   x = 1
   y = 1 / 0
   x = 1

Done:
   Exit Sub
last:
   MsgBox "The following error has been encountered: " & Err.Description

End Sub

When executed, it gives the following result:

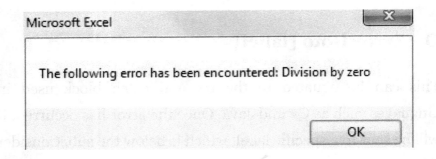

Microsoft Excel

The following error has been encountered: Division by zero

OK

When an error has occurred, the VBA will go to the section named "last". This is what the "On Error GoTo last" statement specifies. When VBA finds the "y = 1 / 0", an error is found and it jumps to the "last" section.

The use of "Err.Description" helps us know the kind of error that has occurred, which in this case is "Division by zero", as shown in the output.

On Error Resume Next

This signals the VBA to ignore the error and continue with execution. Although it is useful in certain occasions, you should avoid using it. If you need to ignore the error of division by zero, this is the best error handling technique for you. Consider the code given below:

```
Sub IgnoreError()
    On Error Resume Next

    Dim x As Long, y As Long

    x = 1
    y = 1 / 0
    x = 1
End Sub
```

The code will run and you will not notice that an error has occurred, as it will be ignored. It is not a good approach, as the behavior of the program becomes unpredictable and you may end up getting the wrong result.

Consider the code given below, which shows an ideal example where we can ignore the error:

```vba
Sub IdealApplication()
 On Error Resume Next

  ' Reference needed
  Dim Outlook As Outlook.Application
  Set Outlook = New Outlook.Application

  If Outlook Is Nothing Then
     MsgBox "A Microsoft Outlook session cannot be
created." _
          & " The email won't be sent."
     Exit Sub
  End If
End Sub
```

In this example, we need to check whether or not we have Microsoft Outlook on our computer. Our aim is to know whether it exists or not, but not to get the specific error. Even if an error has occurred, we will continue. We then check for the "Outlook" variable value. If the application is not found, the value of the variable will be "Nothing".

On Error Goto -1

In this error handling statement, the current error is cleared, rather than having to set a default behavior for it. If the error has occurred, then it will have to return to default behavior, which is "On Error Goto 0". In case of occurrence of another error, VBA stops at the current line.

After exiting the sub, the error will automatically be cleared. Consider the example given below:

```
Sub MoreErrors()
    On Error GoTo last

    ' A "Type mismatch" error will be generated
    Error (13)


Done:
    Exit Sub
last:
    ' An "Application-defined" error will be generated
    Error (1034)
End Sub
```

Our first error will make the execution jump to "last" label. Our second error will then stop on the line that has the 1034 error.

Err.Raise

This is used for creation of the errors. It is the best way if you need to create custom errors for your app. For Java and C# developers, this can be equated to the "Throw" statement. It takes the syntax given below:

Err.Raise [error number], [error source], [error description]

Consider the example given below:

Sub CheckWorksheet()

  On Error GoTo last

  If Len(Sheet1.Range("A1")) <> 5 Then
    Err.Raise   ERROR_INVALID_DATA, "CheckWorksheet" _
    , "Cell 1 value must have 5 characters exactly."
  End If

```vba
' continue if the cell has valid data
Dim id As String
id = Sheet1.Range("A1")


Done:
    Exit Sub
last:
    ' Err.Raise will send the code here
    MsgBox "An error has been encountered: " &
Err.Description
End Sub
```

In the above example, we are checking the value contained in cell A1, and this value must have exactly 5 characters. If this is not the case, then an error will be shown!

Err.Clear

This tool is used when we need to clear numbers and text from Err.Object. This means that the description and the number will be cleared. Here is our example:

```vba
Sub TheErrClear()

    Dim count As Long, x As Long
```

```vb
' Continue if the error since we will be checking for
the error number

On Error Resume Next

For x = 0 To 9
    ' generate an error for each second one
    If x Mod 2 = 0 Then Error (13)

    ' Check for the error
    If Err.Number <> 0 Then
        count = count + 1
        Err.Clear
    End If
Next

Debug.Print "The total errors were: " & count
End Sub
```

In the above example, we are getting a count of the number of errors that have occurred. For each odd number, an error will be generated. For each iteration, we check for the error number, and if this number is not 0, then an error will have occurred. Once the error has been countered, the error number has to be set back to zero so as to check for the next error.

Conclusion

We have come to the end of this guide. VBA (Visual Basic for Applications) is easy for anyone to learn. You can use it to create applications that are created using other programming languages such as Java and C#. It is characterized by its ease of use. This language has numerous features and you can take advantage of these to create a good working application. The language is best suitable for creating desktop applications.

In VBA, you can automate some of the actions you do in Microsoft Excel. You can also create macros that can run when a worksheet has taken actions such as closing of the worksheet, entering values into the Excel cells and others. You can create VBA macros that will help you validate the values that are being entered in a certain Excel worksheet. This shows how important VBA is and why it's a great idea to learn about it, which hopefully this book has assisted you in doing.